Insects
Around the House

by D. M. Souza

 Carolrhoda Books, Inc./Minneapolis

*Many of the photos in this book show the insects larger
than life size. The degree of magnification varies.*

Library of Congress Cataloging-in-Publication Data

Souza, D. M.
    Insects around the house / by D. M. Souza.
        p.   cm.
    Includes index.
    Summary: Describes the life cycles and habits of various
insects found in the house, including the termite, housefly,
and cockroach.
    ISBN 0-87614-438-5
    1. Insects—Juvenile literature. 2. Insect pests—Juvenile
literature. 3. Household pests—Juvenile literature. [1. Insects.
2. Insect pests.]
I. Title.
QL467.2.S68   1991
595.7'065—dc20   90-38290
                                               CIP
                                                AC

Manufactured in the United States of America

1 2 3 4 5 6 7 8 9 10 00 99 98 97 96 95 94 93 92 91

The tropical walking stick may be over a foot long.

Insects Around the House

There are billions of insects living on earth today, more than all other animals combined. A meadow may be a miniature jungle of them. Ten thousand can easily live on 3 square feet of earth. Hundreds may be crawling around outside of your house. A few may be hiding inside.

Some insects are so small you may not be able to see them. Imagine a beetle tiny enough to slip through the eye of a needle. Another insect, the tropical walking stick, may be over a foot long.

An insect's body is divided into three main parts.

An insect is really an inside-out creature. Its skeleton is outside its body, in the form of a coat of armor made of a material called **chitin** (KAI-tin). The skeleton is not only hard but also lightweight and tough. It supports the body, while flexible joints allow it to move around easily.

This body is divided into three main parts: a head, a **thorax**—to which wings and legs are attached—and an **abdomen**, a long, tail-like section.

On top of the insect's head is a pair of **antennae** (an-TEN-ee), or feelers. These antennae are very important to the insect because they may help it smell, hear, or communicate. This may be why insects spend considerable time cleaning their antennae with one or more of their six legs.

An insect's antennae are very important to it.

5

Some insects look small and frail, but they actually have muscles that help them perform incredible tasks. While an elephant may be able to drag an object twice its own weight, the worker honeybee can pull an object 20 times its weight.

You and I have two simple eyes, but some insects have three. Most also have two **compound eyes** that are made up of hundreds, sometimes thousands, of **lenses**. Each compound eye is very sensitive to the slightest movement and can see what the other compound eye cannot.

Most insects have two pairs of wings, strengthened with little tubes called veins. Some insects, however, such as flies, midges, and mosquitoes, have only one pair. Fleas, silverfish, and some members of the ant and termite families have no wings at all.

There is hardly anything that does not serve as food for one kind of insect or another. All have special mouthparts that help them bite, chew, or sip a meal.

Grasshoppers, for example, have jawlike structures called **mandibles** (MAN-dih-buhlz) between their upper and lower lips that move from side to side like scissors. These mandibles help the insect cut and grind plants for food.

Butterflies and moths do not have mandibles. Instead, they have long tubes called **proboscises** (pro-BAH-sis-ehz). When these insects land on a flower, they uncurl their tubes, thrust them deep into the "throat" of the flower, and sip its nectar. As they fly away, the tubes curl up again under their heads.

Insects such as horseflies use their mouthparts to slice into an animal's skin to make blood flow. Then they use spongelike organs to soak up their dinners.

Left: *Butterflies and moths keep their proboscises curled up when not in use.*

Right: *Insects like to eat a variety of things.*

Do you enjoy the taste of hamburgers, hot dogs, and apple pie? What about carpets, wood, books, sweaters, and socks? Well, some insects around your house may actually be eating these and other things—and causing a lot of damage too. Let's take a closer look at a few of these insects, their habits, and their unusual appetites.

Reproductive termites such as the one pictured here are the only termites that have wings.

Under the Front Steps

On a warm spring day, a cloud of insects suddenly rises out of the ground. Hundreds fly into the air. They may look like large ants with wings, but they are actually termites, and it is moving day in their underground colony.

These flying termites, called reproductives, are special. Their only task in life is to produce young, or **larvae** (LAR-vee). Today they are on a flight to start new colonies of their own. After landing, they shed their wings, mate, and look for a nesting place.

One pair chooses a crack near the base of a dead tree. Another finds a fallen log. Still another hollows out a spot in a damp corner under the front steps of a house.

Here the female, or queen, begins laying her eggs, and the male, or king, stays close by to help with the care of their young. Throughout her life, the queen will stay in her royal chamber. Workers will feed her and care for the steady stream of eggs she will lay.

A group of reproductive termites on some rotting wood.

Some queens lay thousands of eggs a year. Others lay thousands in a day and may do so for 20 years, which is much longer than most insects live. Each of these eggs will hatch into a termite that belongs to one of several groups.

One group is made up of blind, wingless workers. They collect food, wait on the royal couple, and build or enlarge the underground tunnels as the colony grows.

Worker termites are blind and wingless.

Soldier termites defend the colony.

Another group consists of soldiers. These termites have large heads and powerful jaws that they use when invaders threaten the safety of the group. They too are blind and wingless. As they move about in search of enemies, they snap their jaws together. Sometimes, to warn others, they knock their heads against wood, making loud sounds.

Some of the royal couple's offspring are born with eyes and wings. These are reproductives, the princes and princesses that will one day fly away and become the kings and queens of new colonies.

The favorite food of all termites is wood.

The principal food of all termites is wood, which workers find with their sense of smell. Termites can make a feast out of fence posts, telephone poles, paper, baseball bats, or houses. They cannot, however, digest the wood. They carry around microscopic creatures called **protozoa** (proh-toh-ZOH-uh) in their digestive systems that do the job for them. These protozoa live only in termites, who are born with them. If the protozoa did not break down the wood fibers and turn them into digestible sugar, the termites would soon die of starvation.

14

When termites' new homes are underground and their food supply is aboveground, they must build passageways. These are built from the inside out and consist of wood and earth particles cemented together with saliva. The finished passageways look like narrow chimneys. They allow workers to move back and forth without being exposed to the outside air. Because termites live in a moist, protected place, they have no need of a hard outer skeleton, or **exoskeleton** (EHKS-oh-skeh-leh-ton). Their bodies are therefore soft and delicate and would shrivel up if exposed to dry air for very long.

As the colony under the house grows larger, more and more mouths must be fed. Slowly the termites nibble away at the wooden supports under the front stairs. Soon the supports become hollow. Each day people walk up and down the stairs and children jump and play on them until they become weaker and weaker. Finally one day, something heavy is carried into the house, and the entire stairway collapses under the weight.

Termites' bodies are soft and delicate.

Every year termites do millions of dollars worth of damage to buildings, and most of the time no one even knows they are present. Although they live almost everywhere, termites are found in greatest numbers in hot climates. There they build mounds 20 to 30 feet aboveground that look like giant mushrooms or pyramids. Termites also live in forests, where they help clear away dead trees and vegetation. For millions of years they have been turning over the soil and helping to enrich the earth. Is it their fault if once in a while the dead wood they eat turns out to be someone's house?

Termites can do a great deal of damage to houses and other buildings.

Giant silkworm moths such as this luna moth may have wingspans as large as 6 inches.

Caps, Carpets, Cornmeal

Turn on a light on a summer night, open a window or door, and watch what happens. In a short time, insects of different sizes and colors will be darting toward the light. Many will be moths, which like to play around lights even though they hide from sunlight.

Some will be very small, with wingspans no wider than the tip of a pen. Others such as the giant silkworm moth measure 4 to 6 inches from one wing to the other.

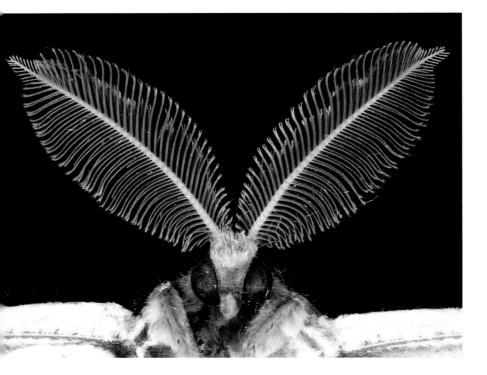

Most moths have feathery antennae like this moon moth does.

Most moths have fat, hairy bodies and feathery antennae. They spend much of their time outdoors, sipping juice from various plants and flowers. Females also search indoors and out for the special foods their young like to eat, and on these foods they lay their eggs.

The young that hatch from the eggs are called **caterpillars** and look more like tiny worms than moths. The word *caterpillar* means hairy cat and describes the young of both moths and butterflies.

Caterpillars have tremendous appetites. Unlike their parents, they do not sip their meals. Instead, they have powerful mandibles that let them bite and chew leaves, the bark of trees, fruit, and many other things. You may have found one munching on an apple or an ear of corn. Some even like to feast on sweaters, blankets, socks, or carpets.

Many caterpillars are beautiful, but their eating habits may be damaging to plants, trees, or clothing.

If a clothes moth finds its way into your house, it may fly into your closet and lay its eggs on your woolen hat. When its young hatch, they immediately begin eating parts of the hat. As they move across the wool, they leave behind a trail of silk threads.

Many caterpillars are able to spin silk from their mouths. Just as you and I have glands that produce saliva in our mouths, these caterpillars have glands that produce liquid silk. The silk is stored in the caterpillar's body until it is ready to make a **cocoon**, or shelter, for itself. Then the silk is forced out through small openings in its mouth and immediately hardens into a strong thread.

A cecropia moth caterpillar has made a cocoon around itself.

This clothes moth caterpillar is eating a blanket. It will leave holes in the blanket when it's done.

As the caterpillars on your cap eat, they grow quickly. Soon their outer coverings become too small for their bodies, so the caterpillars shed them, or **molt**. They do this several times before reaching full size. Then they spin thick webs of silk over themselves and enter what is known as the **pupal stage**.

The word *pupa* means "doll." Inside the silk cocoon, the young moths seem as lifeless as dolls, but changes are taking place. In a short time, adult moths appear. When they fly away, they leave behind their silk cases—and several holes in your cap.

Another moth that may find its way into your home is the Indian meal moth. It is about ¾ of an inch wide, with dust-gray wings streaked with red. It lays its eggs on dried seeds, nuts, flour, cornmeal, and rice. Sometime you might open a package of flour that has been on the shelf for a long time, and tiny moths will fly out. Adult moths sometimes lay their eggs on food before it is packaged. The caterpillars hatch and begin eating. Then, when they change into moths, they find themselves sealed in a package.

While caterpillars do a lot of damage both inside and outside our houses, birds always delight in finding them. Not only do they make a delicious meal for the feathered animals, but they also provide extra nutrition for the birds' young.

A housefly is a common sight inside and outside the house.

From Garbage to Apple Pie

A warm, sweet-smelling pie is cooling on the kitchen table. High above it, a pair of insect wings beats more than two hundred times a second and red-brown eyes bulge in a black head. The black-striped body has shades of yellow on its sides.

The insect lands on the ceiling and begins walking upside down. On the bottom of its feet are pads covered with hairs. From these pads oozes a sticky fluid that makes it possible for the creature to walk anywhere. This insect is a common housefly.

Suddenly its two short, thick antennae detect the warm air moving up from the pie. The housefly zooms down for a landing on the table and begins walking around. The lower parts of its legs tell it when it is nearing the treat. It especially likes warm, sweet food.

Houseflies like almost every type of food.

A female housefly has laid her eggs on this piece of spoiled liver.

Because it has no jaws and cannot chew, the housefly must first turn the pastry into a liquid. To do this, it coughs up a little of its last liquid meal, mixes this with some saliva, and slowly begins softening a morsel of pie.

Clinging to the hairs on its body are bits of dirt, spoiled meat, and rotting vegetables that it picked up outside in the garbage can. There it laid a cluster of about one hundred long, white eggs. Usually the female likes to deposit her eggs on anything rich in bacteria, which is what her young like to eat.

If the weather is warm, the eggs will hatch in 8 to 12 hours into wormlike **maggots**. After eating their egg cases, these maggots feed on everything around them. In 4 or 5 days, they turn into **pupae** (PYOO-pee) and remain in this stage for about the same number of days. Finally they turn into adults and begin laying eggs of their own in 3 to 30 days, depending on the weather.

These are maggots, the larvae of flies.

*You won't want to
share your food with
a housefly.*

Scientists once estimated that if a single female housefly laid her eggs in spring and all of them hatched, by fall there would be as many as five trillion more flies. Luckily, birds, lizards, and other insects eat large numbers of fly eggs, maggots, and adult flies.

A single housefly can carry millions of germs, not only on the hairs on its body but inside its digestive system as well. Because of this, it is responsible for spreading many serious diseases, such as typhoid, cholera, dysentery, and salmonella. One minute it lands on some dung out in the yard, and a few minutes later it lands on your pie in the kitchen.

The next time you hear one of these insects buzzing around the house, shoo it toward an open window or door. Outside, it can help decompose the garbage or bits of food lying around the neighborhood. Inside, you can enjoy a germ-free piece of apple pie.

Have you ever seen a cockroach in your kitchen?

Anything and Everything

Picture yourself coming home from the store with a bag of groceries. You empty out milk, lettuce, oranges, and two loaves of bread and put the bag away in a closet. Hiding on the bottom of the sack is something you did not see. It is a dark brown insect with a broad, flat body, six legs, wings, and two very long antennae. It's a cockroach. This insect likes to hide in dark places. It has learned to survive by eating anything and everything, even its own relatives.

The cockroach in the sack reaches out in all directions with its antennae, trying to detect movement around it. If it is a female cockroach, she will make sure she is alone, then begin laying eggs. She lays about 12 eggs in double rows in a long capsule inside her abdomen. Slowly this capsule stretches out from the end of her body. As it does, the cockroach releases a clear liquid that covers the capsule and hardens around it like cement.

Female cockroaches lay their eggs in capsules that extend out from their bodies.

Cockroaches will eat anything they can find. These cockroaches are nibbling on a potato.

When the cockroach scurries out of the bag, the egg capsule remains attached to the end of her body. She will carry it around with her for about a month. When her young are almost ready to hatch, she will drop the capsule in a dark, safe place and leave.

After another month, the young are ready to hatch, and they struggle to get out of the case. Soon their wiggling and struggling forces the capsule to open like a purse, and out they tumble. Except for the fact that they have no wings, young cockroaches look like their parents and, like their parents, are able to move with unbelievable speed.

During the day, cockroaches hide in drawers, cracks in the floor or walls, or behind window frames. At night they come out in search of a meal. Because they are not fussy eaters they nibble on anything they can find—paper, clothing, bedding, bits of food, garbage or dirt, even bedbugs. Sometimes they leave an unpleasant smell on things they touch.

It will take the young cockroach almost a year to become an adult, and during that time it will go through a series of molts, in which it sheds its outgrown body covering. When a female is fully grown, she will begin laying her own eggs, and as many as four hundred thousand new cockroaches may be hatched in a year's time.

Cockroaches use their antennae and cerci to warn them when danger is near.

Although these insects have two pairs of wings, they seldom use them. Instead, they rely on their long, thin legs to make quick escapes. They are among the fastest runners in the insect world and have a built-in alarm system that warns them when danger is near. It consists of the long antennae on their heads and a pair of short structures on the other end of their bodies. These are called **cerci** (SUHR-see) and are sensitive to the slightest puff of air.

Cockroaches have survived for more than 200 million years by adapting to many different conditions. Long ago they crept under the thick vegetation that once covered the earth. If the weather turned cold, they found warm places to hide. When humans built shelters filled with good things to eat, cockroaches moved inside. Who can blame them for doing that?

Cockroaches have lived on earth for millions of years. They can live in a variety of conditions.

This silverfish can live on the paste that holds a book together.

Insects, Insects Everywhere

Perhaps you have already spotted these or other insects moving around your house. You may have watched an army of ants enter a room on a hot summer day and wondered where they came from or where they were going. You may have seen a slender silverfish race across the bottom of your bathtub or streak across the page of a book. Perhaps you have seen other strange or fascinating insects hiding in a drawer or under the kitchen sink or even running around your bed.

Each year, new insects that no one even knew existed are discovered. Sometimes people stumble upon them accidentally. At other times scientists catch them by putting out dishes of water or jars of food. Sometimes they use different colored lights to attract them.

You might like to try doing something like this. Who knows? You may discover an insect that no one has ever seen before, or one that no one suspected lived in your city or state. Happy insect hunting!

If you've been for a walk in the woods, you might bring a tick such as this one home with you.

Scientists who study animals group them together according to their similarities and differences. Animals that have certain features in common are placed in the same **order**. For example, insects in the same order may go through similar stages before they reach adulthood, or they may have the same kind of mouthparts or the same number of wings. There are about 25 orders of insects in all. The orders of some of the insects discussed in this book are described below.

ORDER	MEANING	EXAMPLES	TYPE OF MOUTHPARTS	NUMBER OF WINGS	WHERE USUALLY FOUND
Diptera	two wings	flies, mosquitoes	larvae: chewing adults: piercing-sucking	2	around plants, animals, food, and garbage
Isoptera	equal wings	termites	chewing	4	in ground and in wood
Lepidoptera	scale wings	moths, butterflies	larvae: chewing adults: piercing-sucking	4	wherever plants grow and in clothes and carpets
Orthoptera	straight wings	cockroaches, grasshoppers, mantids	chewing	4	on plants, in ground, and in houses

Glossary

abdomen: the back section of an insect's body

antennae: a pair of organs on an insect's head that help it sense things around it

caterpillars: the larvae of moths and butterflies

cerci: a pair of sense organs on the back end of certain insects, such as cockroaches

chitin: a hard material from which the skeletons of insects are made

cocoon: a protective case in which some young insects develop

compound eyes: eyes made up of many tiny lenses

exoskeleton: the hard skeleton on the outside of an insect's body

larvae: the young of some insects

lenses: a part of the eye that helps the eye to see

maggots: the larvae of certain insects such as flies and fleas

mandibles: mouthparts that some insects use to chew

molt: to shed skin

order: a group of animals with a number of features in common

proboscises: the mouthparts of certain insects, such as butterflies

protozoa: tiny creatures that live inside some insects and other animals

pupal stage: a stage of insect development between birth and adulthood

pupae: insects in the pupal stage

thorax: the middle section of an insect's body

Index

The photographs are reproduced through the courtesy of: pp. 3, 11, 14, © John
Serrao; pp. 4, 34, © Gregory K. Scott; pp. 5, 17, © Gerry Lemmo; pp. 7, 12, 13, 24,
29, 36, Dwight R. Kuhn; pp. 8, 9, 10, 15, 16, 18, 21, 25, 30, 31, 32, front cover (inset)
© Robert and Linda Mitchell; p. 19, Donald L. Rubbelke; front cover (background),
back cover, William H. Allen, Jr.